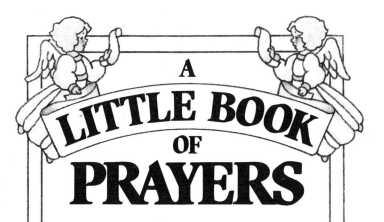

A
LITTLE BOOK
OF
PRAYERS

ILLUSTRATED BY
ROMA BISHOP

Little, Brown and Company
Boston   Toronto

First U.S. edition

Produced by Templar Publishing Ltd,
107 High Street, Dorking, Surrey, England, RH4 1QA.

This edition copyright © Templar Publishing 1987
Illustrations copyright © Templar Publishing 1986

First published 1986 by Hutchinson Children's Books.
An imprint of Century Hutchinson Ltd,
Brookmount House, 62–65 Chandos Place, Covent Garden,
London, England, WC2N 4NW.

Set in Century Schoolbook by Kalligraphics Ltd

Library of Congress Cataloging-in-Publication Data

A Little book of prayers.
    Reprint. Originally published: Surrey: Templar Pub.,
1986.
    Summary: A collection of short prayers which includes
traditional favorites and new ones for pets, friends,
holidays, and comfort.
    1. Prayers – Juvenile literature. 2. Children –
Prayer-books and devotions – English. [1. Prayer books
and devotions] I. Bishop, Roma, ill.
BV265.L49   1987   242'.82   86–27570
ISBN 0–316–09660–1

Color separations by Positive Colour Ltd, Maldon, Essex.
Printed by L.E.G.O., Vicenza, Italy.

Published simultaneously in Canada
by Little, Brown & Company (Canada) Limited

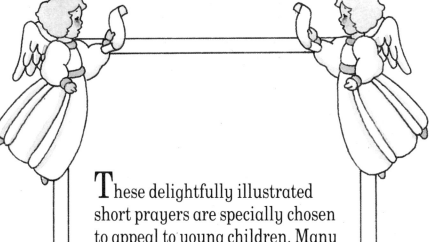

These delightfully illustrated short prayers are specially chosen to appeal to young children. Many are traditional childhood favorites. Some, notably the much-loved "Day by day" prayer, written by St Richard of Chichester, date back centuries. The collection also includes new prayers composed for small children. There are prayers for every occasion, ranging from thanksgiving for family fun, friends, holidays and pets, to prayers of reassurance about night-time fears or illness.

Dear Father, hear and bless
Thy beasts and singing birds,
And guard with tenderness
Small things that have no words.

Be near me, Lord Jesus;
    I ask thee to stay
Close by me for ever,
    and love me, I pray.
Bless all the dear children
    in thy tender care,
And fit us for heaven
    to live with thee there.

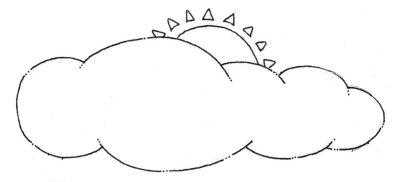

Forgive us, God, for the bad things we
have said and done.

Help us to be kind again to one another
instead.

Give us your spirit so that we may live
happily together in this beautiful world
you have given us.

And please make people in every land love
their enemies as well as their friends.

God set the world in families,
And families in nations,
That we might learn to live as one
By living with relations.

If you and I can make our home
A friendly sort of place,
Then we could make one family
Of all the human race.

The black keys and the white keys
Could all their music bring,
And we'd play a tune together
For everyone to sing.

Dear God,
    thank you for my pets.
I love to play with them
    and stroke their soft fur.
Please don't let me forget
    to feed and care for them.
And by loving them, let me learn
    to love and be kind to others too.

Day by day, dear Lord,
Of Thee three things I pray –
To see Thee more clearly,
To love Thee more dearly,
Follow Thee more nearly,
Day by day.

We thank you, Lord of Heaven,
For all the joys that greet us,
For all that you have given
To help us and delight us
In earth and sky and seas;
The sunlight on the meadows,
The rainbow's fleeting wonder,
The clouds with cooling shadows,
The stars that shine in splendor –
We thank you, Lord, for these.

For swift and gallant horses,
For lambs in pastures springing,
For dogs with friendly faces,
For birds with music thronging
Their chantries in the trees;
For herbs to cool our fever,
For flowers of field and garden,
For bees among the clover
With stolen sweetness laden –
We thank you, Lord, for these.

Lord, keep us safe this night,
Secure from all our fears.
May angels guard us while we sleep,
Till morning light appears.

Dear Jesus, I have a mother and
    father who love me.
But I know that some children are
    all alone in the world.
Please take special care of them so
    that they may have happy
    lives.
Please help me, too – to give
    thanks for my own family.
Bless us all with your love.

Lord Jesus, help me to be brave
and cheerful when I am ill.
Help me to remember all the other
people who are ill or in pain,
and to pray for them.
Give us all your strength and help,
so we may get better soon.

Thank you for the beasts so tall,
Thank you for the creatures small.
Thank you for all things that live,
Thank you, God, for all you give.

Thank you, God, for this new day
In my school to work and play.
Please be with me all day long,
In every story, game and song.
May all the happy things we do
Make you, our Father, happy too.

19

Lord of all hopefulness,
Lord of all joy,
Whose trust ever child-like,
no cares could destroy,
Be there at our waking,
and give us, we pray,
Your bliss in our hearts,
Lord, at the break of the day.

Lord of all gentleness,
Lord of all calm,
Whose voice is contentment,
whose presence is balm,
Be there at our sleeping,
and give us, we pray,
Your peace in our hearts,
Lord, at the end of the day.

Jesus, tender Shepherd, hear me,
Bless thy little lamb tonight;
Through the darkness be thou near me,
Watch my sleep till morning light.

All this day thy hand has led me,
And I thank thee for thy care;
Thou hast clothed me, warmed and fed me,
Listen to my evening prayer.

Let my sins be all forgiven,
Bless the friends I love so well;
Take me, when I die, to heaven,
Happy there with thee to dwell.

Thank you for the world so sweet,
Thank you for the things we eat,
Thank you for the birds that sing,
Thank you, God, for everything.

Thank you, God, for the snow.
It fell softly and silently all
    through the night, and now
    everything is white and
    beautiful.
Help us to be quiet enough to hear
    your voice speaking to us, and
    to obey it always.

O Father of goodness,
We thank you each one
For happiness, healthiness,
Friendship and fun,
For good things we think of
And good things we do,
And all that is beautiful,
Loving and true.

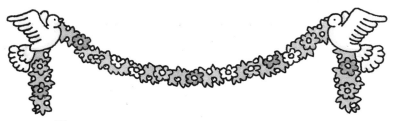

Lord, teach me, that my heart may be
A little house that's fit for Thee –
A house of shining window panes,
Clean from all smears and smuts and stains,
No blinds drawn darkly down, to hide
The things that lie and lurk inside,
And creep and mutter in the night;
For honesty is free as light.
So I will take my broom, and clear
Every dishonest thought, and fear,
And deed right out, that I may be
A little house that's fit for Thee.

Matthew, Mark, Luke and John,
Bless the bed that I lie on.
Four corners to my bed,
Four angels there be spread,
One at the head,
One at the feet,
And two to guard me
While I sleep.

Matthew, Mark, Luke and John,
Bless the bed that I lie on.

God be in my head,
and in my understanding;
God be in my eyes,
and in my looking;
God be in my mouth,
and in my speaking;
God be in my heart,
and in my thinking;
God be at my end,
and at my departing.

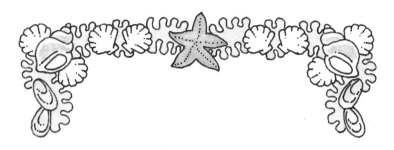

Praise to God, for long, hot summer days
and vacation fun at the seaside.
Thank you for giving us the sunshine and
the blue, sparkling sea.
Thank you for the summer sky and the soft,
golden sand.
Thank you for the seagulls flying overhead
and the sound of children laughing.
Help us to remember these things when we
are sad so that they may make us happy
again.

ACKNOWLEDGMENTS

We would like to thank all those who have given us permission to include their prayers in this book. Every effort has been made to trace and contact copyright owners. If there are any inadvertent omissions in the acknowledgments we apologize to those concerned.

Blandford Press Ltd: Pages 8/9, and 28 by M.E. Procter from *Junior Teacher's Assembly Book*.

Church House Publishing: Page 17, by M. Widdows from *In Excelsis*.

David McKay Company, Inc: Page 14, by Tasha Tudor from *First Prayers*.

Frederick Muller Ltd: Page 4, from *Hymns and Prayers for Children*.

The National Society for Promoting Religious Education: Page 24, by Mrs E. Rutter Leatham from *Hymns and Songs for Children*.

Oxford University Press: Pages 12/13 and 20/21, by Jan Struther (1901–1953) from *Enlarged Songs of Praise*. Three verses omitted by permission.